The Story of a Special Day
Volume 5

January
5

The 5th day of the year, with 360 days (361 in leap years) remaining until the end of the year.

by Michael Dobson

Timespinner
Press

This book is also available in e-book form for Kindle, e-pub devices, and other formats from your favorite online booksellers.

For more information about the series, about us, or about your special day, please email us at editor@timespinnerpress.com.

Look for other volumes in *The Story of a Special Day,* coming often. See www.timespinnerpress.com for details and for the most recent information.

Table of Contents

For the definition of "O.S.," "CE," and "BCE" used with some dates , see the section "On Names and Dates."

Cover: San Francisco's Golden Gate Bridge, by "Francis1203"— the EVENT OF THE DAY.

Quote of the Day

"In view of the fact that God limited
the intelligence of man, it seems unfair
that he did not also limit his stupidity."

Konrad Adenauer, born January 5, 1876

Today in History

January 5

The Golden Gate Bridge, by Chesley Bonestell

Event of the Day
Golden Gate Bridge

On January 5, 1933, construction of San Francisco's iconic Golden Gate Bridge began. Declared one of the Wonders of the Modern World by the American Society of Civil Engineers, the 1.7 mile long bridge connects the northern edge of the city of San Francisco to Marin County. From its opening in 1937 until 1964, it was the longest suspension bridge in the world.

Prior to the construction of the bridge, people crossed San Francisco Bay by ferryboat. Although a bridge had been long desired, it wasn't until 1916 that engineering student Joseph Strauss developed a groundbreaking cantilever design for his graduate thesis. Originally estimated to cost $100 million ($2.12 billion in 2009 dollars), the bridge faced much controversy, especially from the owners of the ferry service. Because Strauss was relatively inexperienced, other engineers and designers were added to the project and designed many of its most iconic elements.

In spite of the original high price tag, the actual construction was budgeted at $35 million but came in $1.3 million under budget! On opening day, some 200,000 people crossed the bridge either on foot or on roller skates; cars were permitted the following day. An official song, "There's a Silver Moon on the Golden Gate," celebrated the opening, and from

Washington, DC, President Franklin D. Roosevelt pressed a button to begin official vehicle traffic over the bridge.

The Golden Gate Bridge is featured in many films, documentaries, and even video games set in San Francisco. It is notorious for the number of suicides; it is the second-most used suicide site/suicide bridge in the world, with over 1,600 bodies recovered from people who jumped from the bridge. (The exact number is no longer published because of the role of publicity in encouraging further attempts.)

With its art deco decorations and brilliant orange vermillion color, the bridge was designed with aesthetics in mind as well as safety. It is no wonder that this beautiful work remains one of the world's most famous bridges.

A US Navy aircraft carrier passes under the bridge

The Golden Gate Bridge in 1984

Illustration from the court-martial of Alfred Dreyfus

What Happened on January 5?

From the creation of great works of engineering and art, to devastating wars and natural disasters, thousands of years of history have left their mark on each and every day of the year. Here are some important events that occurred on January 5.

1066 — A **succession crisis** following the death of Edward the Confessor begins the events that will lead to the Norman conquest of England later that year.

1757 — French king Louis XV survives an **assassination attempt**. The assassin becomes the last person in France executed by drawing and quartering.

1781 — During the **American Revolutionary War**, British forces led by Benedict Arnold burn the city of Richmond, Virginia.

1895 — French army officer **Alfred Dreyfus** is convicted of treason and sentenced to life imprisonment on Devil's Island, although he swears he is innocent. His unjust conviction becomes a major scandal, known as the Dreyfus affair. He is finally exonerated and released in 1906.

1911 — The largest black fraternity, **Kappa Alpha Psi (ΚΑΨ)**, is founded at Indiana University.

1914 — The **Ford Motor Company** implements a "living wage" policy, paying all workers a minimum of $5 for an eight-hour day.

1919 — The *Deutsche Arbeiterpartei* (German Worker's Party) is founded. A young Adolf Hitler joins and soon takes over the organization, changing its name to the *Nationalsozialistische Deutsche Arbeiterpartei,* more commonly known as the **Nazi Party.**

1925 — Nellie Tayloe Ross is sworn in as governor of Wyoming, the **first woman ever to serve as governor** of a US state.

1968 — The **Prague Spring,** a period of political liberalization in Communist-dominated Czechoslovakia begins. It lasts until the Soviets invade in August of that year.

1991 — The **United States Embassy in Mogadishu**, Somalia, is evacuated by helicopter airlift during the Somali Civil War.

2005 — The **dwarf planet Eris** is discovered. Originally called the "tenth planet" because it is outside the orbit of Pluto, it was reclassified (along with Pluto) to dwarf planet status in 2006.

Neillie Tayloe Ross

Quote of the Day

"Difficulties are just things to overcome, after all."

Ernest Shackleton, died January 5, 1922

Births
and
Deaths

THER
ACA
MAGNA

January 5

Sonny Bono (left) with Cher from the *Sonny and Cher Show*.
Sonny Bono died January 5, 1988

Notable January 5 People

With the current world population at about seven billion people, on average about 19 million people also celebrate their birthdays on January 5 — and that isn't counting millions and millions who came before! No matter when you were born, you share your birthday with many special people whose accomplishments (and occasionally embarrassments) have been noted as part of history.

In this section, you'll meet fascinating people who share your birthday. They're organized by what they're famous for, and then in reverse chronological order from most recent to earliest. Those who are shown in photographs or artwork have a box around them. We don't have photos of everyone, so please forgive us if your favorite person is missing.

Some of these people you've heard of, others will be new to you, but they all make up an important part of the reason that January 5 is a truly special day!

Egg McMuffin, invented by Herb Peterson, born January 5, 1919
(Photo: Evan-Amos)

Who Was Born on January 5?

Art and Illustration

Hayao Miyazaki (宮崎 駿), Japanese animation director responsible for such classics as *Princess Mononoke, Spirited Away,* considered one of the greatest animation directors of all time. (1941)

Yves Tanguy, French surrealist painter. (1900)

Business and Economics

Herb Peterson, fast food executive and scientist, invented the McDonald's Egg McMuffin breakfast sandwich. (1919)

King Camp Gillette, inventor of the disposable razor blade and founder of the Gillette Safety Razor Company. (1855)

Jean-Baptiste Say, French economist known for Say's Law of Markets, "Supply creates its own demand," sometimes paraphrased as "If you build it, they will come." (1767)

Government and Politics

Juan Carlos I, King of Spain, helped dismantle the regime of Generalissimo Francisco Franco and establish and constitutional monarchy in his country. (1938)

Walter Mondale, 42nd US Vice President, Democratic nominee for President in 1984, former Senator from Minnesota. **(1928)**

Zulfikar Ali Bhutto, president and prime minister of Pakistan, known as *Quaid-i-Awam* (People's Leader), father of Benazir Bhutto. (1928)

Hosea Williams, American civil rights leader and activist, confidant of Martin Luther King, Jr. (1926)

Konrad Adenauer, first post-World War II chancellor of West Germany, credited with the *Wirtschaftswunder* ("economic miracle") that restored economic prosperity in his country. (1876)

Zulfikar Ali Bhutto (Dutch National Archives)

Journalism and Letters

Charlie Rose, television talk show host and journalist, host of the eponymous *Charlie Rose* show. (1942)

Umberto Eco, novelist and philosopher best known for best-sellers including *The Name of the Rose* and *The Prague Cemetery.* (1932)

Jeane Dixon, astrologer and self-proclaimed psychic, author of a popular national newspaper astrology column. (1904)

Stella Gibbons, author of *Cold Comfort Farm* and other novels. (1902)

Herbert Bayard Swope, journalist and member of the Algonquin Round Table; first recipient of the Pulitzer Prize and coiner of the phrase "Cold War."(1882)

Military and Exploration

Harold Gatty, navigator on board the Lockheed Vega *Winnie Mae*, piloted by Wiley Post, which set a record for aerial circumnavigation of the world in 1931. (1903)

Harold Gatty (right) with Wiley Post in front of the aircraft Winnie Mae (German Federal Archives)

Captain Stephen Decatur, USN, by John Wesley Jarvis)

Stephen Decatur, youngest man ever to reach the rank of Captain in the US Navy. He is often remembered for an after-dinner toast he gave in 1816, in which he said, "Our country—in her intercourse with foreign nations, may she always be in the right, and always successful, right or wrong," often misquoted as "My country, right or wrong." (1779)

Zebulon Pike, American general and explorer best known as the namesake of Colorado's Pike's Peak. He led expeditions exploring the recently acquired Louisiana Territory at the same time as the more famous Lewis and Clark Expedition. He was killed in the Battle of York during the War of 1812. (1778)

Music and Dance

Marilyn Manson (Brian Warner), known as the front man of the band of the same name, nominated for four Grammy Awards. (1969)

Carrie Ann Inaba, dancer and choreographer best known for her work on the TV series *Dancing with the Stars.* (1968)

Chris Stein, co-founder and lead guitarist of the new wave band Blondie. (1950)

Phil Ramone, record producer, winner of 14 Grammy awards, who produced a wide range of artists including Ray Charles, Bob Dylan, Barbra Streisand, Simon & Garfunkel, Frank Sinatra, and Luciano Pavarotti. (1934)

Alvin Ailey, African-American choreographer and activist, founder of the Alvin Ailey American Dance Theater and winner of the Presidential Medal of Freedom. (1931)

Sam Phillips, founder of Sun Records, discoverer of Elvis Presley as well as such recording artists as Jerry Lee Lewis and Johnny Cash, considered one of the pioneers of rock and roll and rockabilly. (1923)

Arturo Michelangeli,considered one of the greatest classical pianists of the 20th century. (1920)

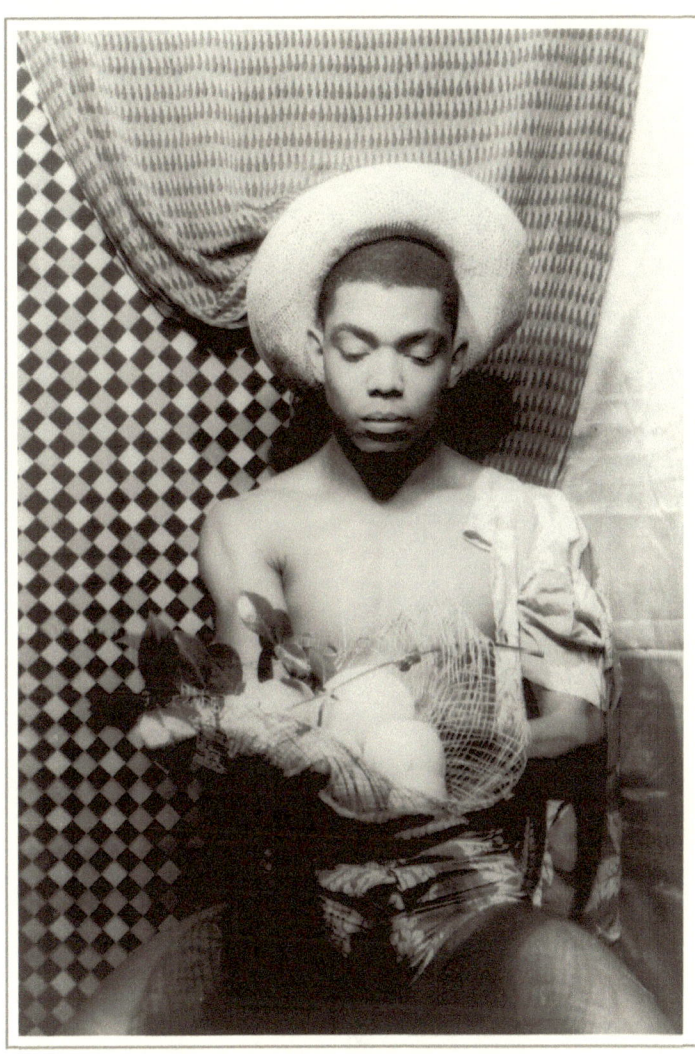

Alvin Ailey (Photo: Carl Van Vechten)

Diane Keaton

Performing Arts

January Jones, actress best known for her role as Betty Draper in the television series *Mad Men.* (1978)

Bradley Cooper, actor and producer known for roles in *Silver Linings Playbook, American Hustle,* and *American Sniper,* receiving four Academy Award nominations as best actor. He was named "Sexiest Man Alive" by *People* Magazine in 2011.

Ricky Paull Goldin, known for his roles in the daytime dramas *All My Children* and *The Bold and the Beautiful.* (1965)

Clancy Brown, actor and voice artist, appeared in the film *The Shawshank Redemption* and as the voice of Mr. Krabs on *SpongeBob SquarePants.* (1959)

Pamela Sue Martin, actress known for her role as Nancy Drew on *The Hardy Boys/Nancy Drew Mysteries,* and as Fallon on the nighttime soap opera *Dynasty.* (1953)

Ted Lange, actor best known for his role as the bartender Isaac in the long-running TV series *The Love Boat.* (1948)

Diane Keaton, film actress known for her partnership with Woody Allen as well as for roles in such films as the *Godfather* trilogy, *Looking for Mr. Goodbar, Reds,* and many others. (1946)

Roger Spottiswoode, directed such films as *Under Fire, Tomorrow Never Dies,* and *Turner & Hooch.* (1945)

Robert Duvall, award-winning actor who appeared in such films as *To Kill a Mockingbird, Godfather I/II, M*A*S*H,* and many others. (1931)

Jane Wyman, actress best known as the first wife of actor and US President Ronald Reagan. Won an Academy Award for her role in 1948's *Johnny Belinda.* (1917)

George Reeves, actor best known for playing the title role in the 1950s television series *Adventures of Superman.* He reportedly committed suicide in 1959, but some suspected murder; the story forms the basis of the 2006 film *Hollywoodland.* (1914)

Hugh Brannum, known for playing "Mr. Green Jeans" on the children's television show *Captain Kangaroo.* (1910)

Mr. Green Jeans (Hugh Brannum, left) about to surprise Captain Kangaroo (Bob Keeshan)

Philosophy and Religion

Sivaya Subramuniyaswami, Hindu religious leader known as Gurudeva, honored by the World Religious Parliament as one of five modern-day international religious teachers promoting Hinduism. (1927)

Paramahansa Yogananda, author of *Autobiography of a Yogi,* which introduced the West to meditation and the practice of yoga. (1893)

Rudolf Christoph Euken, German philosopher who won the 1908 Nobel Prize for Literature. (1846)

Francisco Suárez, Jesuit priest, philosopher, and theologian, generally regarded as among the greatest scholastics in Catholic history. (1548)

Science and Medicine

Stephen Cole Kleene, mathematician known as a founder of recursion theory, which is one of the foundations of modern computer science, and developer of numerous mathematical concepts. (1909)

Kathleen Kenyon, called one of the most influential archaeologists of the 20th century, best known for her research and excavations at Jericho. (1906)

 **Agnes von Kurowsky,** American nurse who inspired the character "Catherine Barkley" in Ernest Hemingway's *Farewell to Arms.* (1892)

Hans Eppinger, Austrian physician who experimented on concentration camp prisoners at Dachau, who committed suicide before he could be brought before the Nuremberg Trials. (1879)

Joseph Erlanger, physiologist and neuroscientist who shared the 1944 Nobel Prize in Physiology or Medicine. (1874)

Sports

Warrick Dunn, football running back named NFL Offensive Rookie of the Year in 1997. (1975)

Chuck McKinley, American former World No. 1 men's tennis champion. (1941)

Chuck Noll, football player and coach known for his long tenure with the Pittsburgh Steelers, including four Super Bowl victories, elected to the Pro Football Hall of Fame. (1932)

Dorothy Levitt, known as "The Fastest Girl on Earth," first British woman racing driver, holder of the world's first water speed record and the women's world land speed record, and inventor of the rear-view mirror. (1882)

Dorothy Levitt

Ban Johnson, baseball executive who founded and served as first president of the American League. (1864)

Bob Caruthers, baseball pitcher and right fielder who played primarily for the St. Louis Browns and the Brooklyn Bridegrooms, credited as having the highest winning percentage of any major league pitcher in history. (1864)

Calvin Coolidge

Who Died on January 5?

Business and Economics

Momofuku Ando (安藤 百福), inventor of instant noodles, founder of Nissin Food Products. (2007)

Government and Politics

Tip O'Neill, 47th Speaker of the United States House of Representatives. (1994)

Calvin Coolidge, 30th President of the United States, nicknamed "Silent Cal." (1933)

Samuel Huntington, signer of the US Declaration of Independence, President of the Continental Congress, and Governor of Connecticut. (1796)

Edward the Confessor, King of the English, ruled England for 24 years as the last monarch of the House of Wessex. He was succeeded by Harold, from the rival House of Godwin, who was defeated and killed later the same year by William the Conqueror. Known for his piety, Edward was canonized in 1161 by Pope Alexander III. (1066)

Military and Exploration

Amy Johnson, aviation pioneer, first female pilot to fly alone from Britain to Australia. (1941)

Amy Johnson

Ernest Shackleton, polar explorer who led three expeditions into the Antarctic. On his third expedition, his ship became trapped in ice and was slowly crushed, and the crew traveled over 720 miles in lifeboats to reach safety. (1922)

Photograph from Ernest Shackleton's 1909 expedition to the Antarctic. Shackleton is on the far right.

Joseph Radetzky von Radetz, Czech nobleman who became a field marshal in the Austrian army, serving in the military for more than 70 years. He is the subject of Johann Strauss I's famous composition *Radetzky March.* (1858)

Music and Dance

Pierre Boulez, composer and conductor, received 26 Grammy Awards. (2016)

Danny Sugerman, manager of The Doors and author of several books about the band and lead singer Jim Morrison. (2005)

---

*Sonny Bono, half of the singing duo Sonny & Cher, later mayor of Palm Springs, California and member of the US House of Representatives. *Photo page 12.* (1998)

Burton Lane, composer and lyricist best known for *Finian's Rainbow* and *On a Clear Day You Can See* Forever. He is credited with discovering Judy Garland. (1997)

Mistinguett, French actress and singer (born Jeanne Bourgeois), at one time the highest-paid female entertainer in the world. She had a long relationship with Maurice Chevalier. (1956)

Mistinguett (left) with Maurice Chevalier (Photo: François Vals)

Performing Arts

Arthur Kennedy, actor known for roles in such films as *High Sierra, Lawrence of Arabia, Elmer Gantry,* and many others. (1990)

Hans Conried, actor and voice artist best known for the sitcom *Make Room for Daddy* and as the voice of Captain Hook in Disney's *Peter Pan.* (1978)

Philosophy and Religion

John Neumann, first American bishop (and only male citizen) to be canonized by the Catholic Church. He founded the first Catholic diocesan school system in the US. (1860)

Science and Medicine

Norman Heatley, developer of a key process to purify penicillin efficiently in bulk. (2004)

Harold Urey, physical chemist who won the 1934 Nobel Prize in Chemistry for the discovery of deuterium. He was important in the development of the atomic bomb. (1981)

Max Born, German physicist and mathematician who won the 1954 Nobel Prize in Physics for his research into quantum mechanics. (1970)

George Washington Carver, botanist and inventor, called the "Black Leonardo" by *Time* Magazine, researched and promoted alternative crops to cotton. (1943)

George Washington Carver

Sports

Don Carter, known as "Mr. Bowling," voted #1 among 20th century bowlers in 1999, first athlete of any kind to earn $1 million in a single endorsement deal. (2012)

Pete Maravich, all-time leading NCAA Division I scorer and one of the youngest players ever inducted into the Naismith Memorial Basketball Hall of Fame. (1988)

Rogers Hornsby, baseball infielder, manager, and coach, with a .358 batting average and a single season record of .424. He was named to the Baseball Hall of Fame in 1942. (1963)

Rabbit Maranville, played 23 seasons in the National League, a record that lasted until 1986 . He was inducted into the Baseball Hall of Fame just months after his death. (1954)

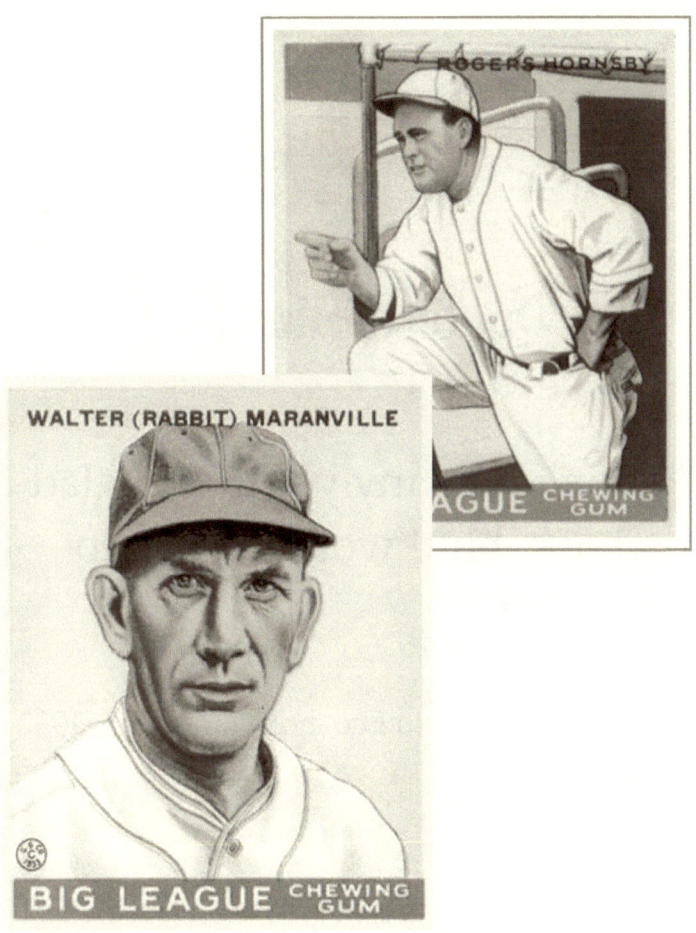

Goudey baseball cards for Rogers Hornsby and Rabbit Maranville

Quote of the Day

"I don't miss my youth. I'm glad I had one, but I wouldn't like to start over."

Umberto Eco, born January 5, 1932

Holidays
Around
the World

January 5

Song poster for "The Twelve Days of Christmas," by Xavier Romero-Frias

Holidays Around the World

If you're looking for a reason to take your special day off, you should know that every single day is a holiday somewhere in the world! Here's what you can celebrate on January 5!

General Events

National Bird Day

On National Bird Day in the United States, people celebrate through birdwatching, studying birds, bird drinking games, and other activities. Bird adoption is also a common activity, as well as educating bird owners about their responsibilities, including issues such as "screaming, biting, constant cleanups, the need for daily interaction and a varied diet." Similar celebrations can be found in other countries; World Migratory Bird Day is celebrated internationally on the second weekend of May each year.

Christmas Season

Twelfth Day and Night of Christmas

Ready for the sound of twelve drummers drumming? For most Western Christian denominations, the "Twelvetide," or Twelve Days of Christmas (celebrated in the famous song), begins on Christmas Day (some begin the day after) and runs until January 5 or 6.

Eastern Orthodox Christians who keep to the old Julian calendar celebrate Christmas on January 7 and the twelve days run through January 19. Various celebrations and religious rites take place during the twelve days, though these vary by denomination.

Eve of the Theophany

In Eastern Orthodox Christianity, January 5 is a day of strict fasting, in which the devout do not eat anything until the first star is seen that night. The Theophany, celebrated the following day, is equivalent to the Epiphany, commemorating either the visit of the Three Magi to the newborn Christ Child (Western Christianity) or the commemoration of the baptism of Jesus in the Jordan River (Eastern Christianity).

Food Holidays

In the United States, almost every day of the year is dedicated to a particular food. Sponsored by manufacturers, retailers, farmers, or simply fans, these days are often proclaimed by the President, Congress, state governors, or mayors. Given that there are more different foods than days of the year, some days honor more than one kind of food!

January 5 is **National Whipped Cream Day.** Whipped cream was initially popularized in the 16th century, when it was called "milk snow." It got its current English name in 1673.

Other countries have official food days, too, but they're not as common. In the United Kingdom, January 5 is **Sausage Day**, and in Japan, it's **Strawberry Day**. One goes better with whipped cream than the other.

In addition, the entire month of January is used to celebrate numerous foods. Here's a list of what to eat in the month of January!

- California Dried Plum Digestive Health Month
- Hot Tea Month
- National Soup Month
- Oatmeal Month

And while we're on the subject of food, it's Be Kind to Food Servers Month in Tennessee.

Christian Feast Days

Each day in the year is considered a feast day for one or more saints. They are somewhat different in western Christianity (Catholicism and many forms of Protestantism) and in eastern (Orthodox) Christianity.

In *Western Christianity*, Charles of Mount Argus, John Neumann (Catholicism), Pope Telesphorus, Simeon Stylites (Latin Church) are commemorated on January 5.

In *Eastern Orthodox Christianity*, it is the commemoration of the Prophet Micah, Saint Sycletia of Alexandria, Saint Apollinaris, Saint Menas of Sinai, Saint Emiliana, Saint Kiara, and Saint Gaudentius of Gnesen. (These are observed on January 18 by "Old Calendarists.")

Honorary Months

Presidents, Congresses, and nations around the world issue proclamations recognizing particular months to honor certain causes. These events generally fall in June, though honorary months do come and go. Holidays established by states and nonprofit organizations are listed if verified. If not otherwise specified, all months are US. There is some variation from year to year; some celebratory months get added and others get dropped. Two places to get up to date information are the current edition of *Chase's Calendar of Events* or the website www.brownielocks.com/january.html.

- Adopt a Rescued Bird Month
- Bath Safety Month
- Be Kind to Food Servers Month
- Birth Defects Month
- California Dried Plum Digestive Month
- Cervical Health Awareness Month
- Financial Wellness Month
- Get Organized Month

- International Child-Centered Divorce Awareness Month
- International Creativity Month

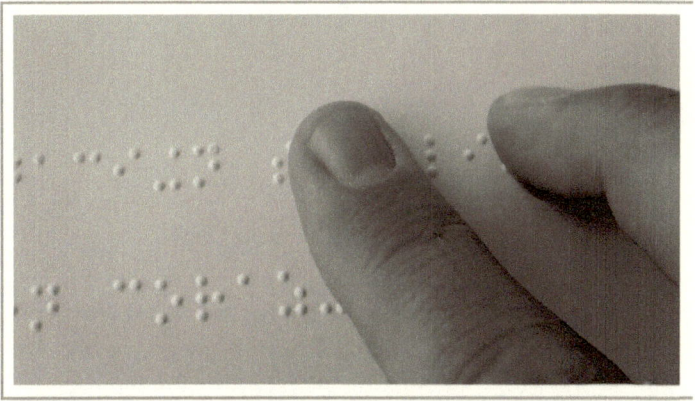

A person reading a braille book, for National Braille Literacy Month
(Photo: Antonio X Alonso)

- **National Braille Literacy Month**
- National Clean Up Your Computer Month
- National Codependency Awareness Month
- National Mentoring Month
- National Polka Music Month
- National Poverty in America Awareness Month
- National Skating Month
- National Soup Month
- National Thank You Month
- National Volunteer Blood Donor Month
- Oatmeal Month

- Slavery and Human Trafficking Prevention Month
- Stalking Awareness Month
- Teen Driving Awareness Month
- Train Your Dog Month (also Walk Your Dog Month)
- Weight Loss Awareness Month

Moveable and Multi-Day Events

Some events take place over a specific week or time period. Start and finish dates may vary from year to year. Some events occur on different days each year (such as "fourth Saturday of a month"). These events sometimes take place on this day.

First Week of January
- Celebration of Life Week
- Diet Resolution Week
- Silent Record Week
- New Year's Resolution Week

Week Long Celebrations that Sometimes Include January 5
- Home Office Safety and Security Week
- National Lose Weight/Feel Great Week
- Elvis's Birthday Celebration Week (week that includes Elvis's birthday, January 8)

1st Friday (can be any day between January 1-7)

- Children's Day (Bahamas)

1st Monday (can be any day between January 1-7)

- Handsel Monday (Scotland and northern England)

Non-Gregorian Events

Not every culture uses the familiar Gregorian calendar, so some events not only shift within a range of a few days depending on the year, but may even migrate through the months. Here is a selection of events around the world that sometimes take place on January 5.

- Dhanurmas (Hindu calendar)
- Thiruvathira (Hinduism, Tamil calendar)
- Lohri (Punjab)
- Thai Pongal (Hinduism, Tamil calendar)
- Mattu Pongal (Hinduism, Tamil calendar)
- Makara Sankranthi (Hinduism)
- Thaipusam (Hinduism, Tamil calendar)
- Tu B'Shevat

Quote of the Day

"It's easy to kill a movie. Just move it to January."

Mike Myers, as "Dr. Evil"
from the *Austin Powers* movies

About the Month of

January

January, by Hans Thoma

January: The First Month

That blasts of January
Would blow you through and through.
> — *William Shakespeare*, The Winter's Tale

January wasn't always the first month in the year. In ancient Rome, March was the first month until about 450 BCE. Even after January became the official first month in the calendar, Romans still counted dates from the inauguration of the consuls, March 15 and May 1.

In the Middle Ages, Christian feast days were used to start the new year, including March 25 and December 25. It wasn't until the 16th century that European nations made January 1 the official start of the new year. (This was called "Circumcision Style" because January 1 was also celebrated as the Feast of the Circumcision of Jesus.)

The name January (*Ianuarius*) is derived from the Roman god Janus, the god of beginning and transitions. Janus gives his name to the Latin word for door (*ianua*), because January is the door to the year. Janus is normally portrayed as having two faces, one looking toward the future and one toward the past. In spite of that, the goddess Juno was the patron of that month.

In both the Julian and Gregorian calendars (see "What Day of the Week..."), January is the first month of the year and one of seven months with 31 days. In the Northern Hemisphere, January is the coldest month of the year, and in the Southern Hemisphere, it's the warmest, equivalent to the Northern Hemisphere's July.

January in Other Cultures

The month of January has different names in different languages. Some nations use calendars other than the Gregorian, and their months may overlap with January. In lunar-based calendars, such as the Islamic calendar, months move through the seasons. Still, many languages often have a word for January itself.

Albanian: Janar

Anglo-Saxon: Wulf-monath

Arabic (Egypt, Sudan, Yemen): يونأغيناير (*yanāyir*)

Arabic (Levant): حزيركانون الثاني (*kānūn al-thānī*)

Arabic (Libya): الصهنار (*aynu n-nār*)

Arabic (Algeria and Tunisia): جأينجانفي (*Jānfī*)

Arabic (Morocco): غيناير (*yanāyər*)

Azerbaijani: Yanvar

Basque: Urtarril

Bulgarian: януари (*januari*)

Chinese: 一月 (Cantonese: *yātyuht*; Mandarin: *yīyuè*; Taiwanese: *it-goeh*)

Corsican: Ghjennaghju

Croatian: Siječanj

Czech: Leden

Finnish: Tammikuu (oak moon)

French: Janvier

German/Danish/Norwegian/Slovenian: Januar

Greek: Ιανουάριος (*Ianouários*)

Haitian Creole: Janvye

Hebrew: ינואר (*yanû'ar*)

Hindi: जनवरी (*janvarī*)

Hungarian: Január

Irish (Gaelic): Eanáir mí Eanáir

Italian: Gennaio

Japanese: 一月 (*ichigatsu*), 睦月 (*mutsuki*)

Kazakh: Қаңтар (*Ķaņtar*)

Korean: 일월 (*ilweol*)

Lithuanian: Sausis

Maori: Kohitātea

Old English: Se æfterra Gēola

Polish: Styczeń

Portuguese: Janeiro

Russian: январь (*janvar'*)

Scottish Gaelic: am Faoilleach

Sesotho: Pherekgong

Slovene: Prosinec

Spanish: Enero

Swahili/Dutch/Swedish: Januari

Swazi: Bhimbidvwane

Thai: มกราคม (*makarakhom*)

Turkish: Ocak

Vietnamese: 腺义 (*tháng một*)
Walloon: Djanvî
Welsh: Ionawr
Yiddish: אויגויאַננואַר (*yanuar*)
Zulu: uJanuwari

Mengapa? Zašto?
为什么呢？
Por quê? Чаму?
Чому?
Poukisa? كيون؟ Per què?
Tại sao? Miks?
Bakit? Kial? למה?
Waarom? Hvers vegna?
どうして？ פֿאַרוואָס? Niyə?
Warum? Dlaczego? Pourquoi?
Ինչու՞? Зашто? چرا! Quid?
Cén fáth? Pam?
Zergatik? როტომ? Miért?
Proč?
Kwa nini? Hoekom? क्यों?
De ce? Kodėl?
เพราะเหตุใด Защо? Why?
Perché? Miksi?
لماذا؟ Prečo? Varför?
Γιατί;
Għaliex? ¿Por qué? Pse?
왜? Почему? Зошто?
Kāpēc? Neden?
Hvorfor? 為什麼呢？

January Sayings and Superstitions

Here are some sayings and superstitions associated with the month of January.

New Year Superstitions

- It's important to kiss those dearest to us at the stroke of the New Year to keep their affections for the next twelve months.

- The new year must not be seen with bare cupboards. Stock up on supplies and make sure there's plenty of money in ever wallet in the home.

- Do not begin the new year with the household in debt.

- The first person to enter your home after the stroke of midnight will tell you the kind of year you will have.

- Do not let anything leave your house on the first day of the year, not even garbage.

- Start your year off with good luck by eating hoppin' john, a dish made with black-eyed peas and rice (southern United States).

- Wear something new on January 1.

- Be sure to open the door at midnight to let the old year escape.

- Babies born on New Year's Day will always have good luck.

January Wedding Superstitions

- A January bride will be a prudent housekeeper, and very good tempered.
- Married in January's hoar and rime / Widowed you'll be before your prime.
- Married when the year is new, he'll be loving, kind and true.

January Symbols

Birthstone: Garnet, representing constancy.

Soviet postage stamp showing a geologist finding garnets

Birth Flower (Britain): Carnation, representing love, fascination, and distinction

Vase with Red and White Carnation on a Yellow Background,
by Vincent van Gogh

Birth Flower (America): Carnation or Snowdrop (*Galanthus*)

A New Year's greeting card with snowdrops

Birth Flower (China): Plum blossom (*prunus mume*)

Red Plum Blossom (Photo: Frank Gualtieri)

Birth Flower (Japan): Camellia

Camellias (Clara Maria Pope)

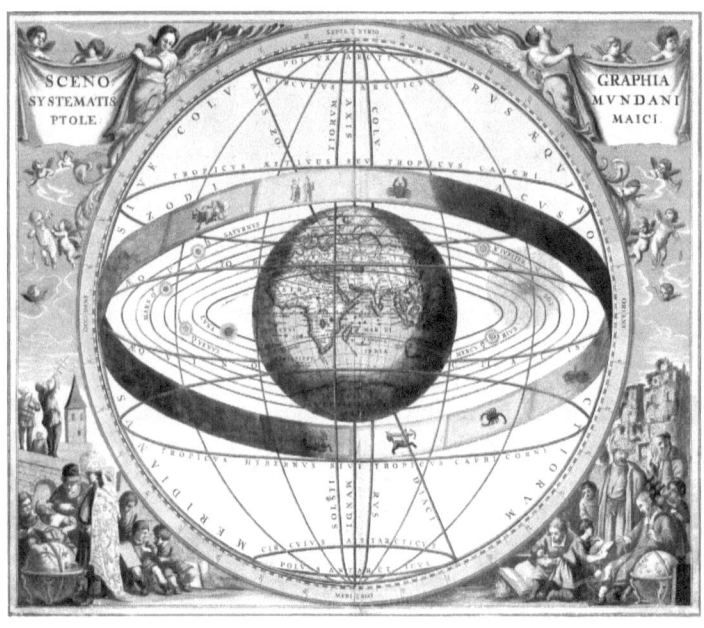

Scenography of the Ptolemaic Cosmography, by Johannes van
Loon, based on Andreas Cellarius's *Harmonia Macrocosmica,* 1660

January Zodiac Signs

From the perspective of someone on Earth, the Sun appears to move through the sky throughout the year, along a path astronomers call the *ecliptic plane*. The ecliptic plane is divided into twelve constellations, known as the zodiac, based on traditionally observed patterns of stars. On your birthday, you can't see your constellation, because it's in the daytime sky.

The zodiac was first developed by Babylonian astronomers about 2,500 years ago. Because they were unaware that the Earth wobbles like a spinning top (known as *precession*), they didn't make allowance for the fact that the Sun's path through the zodiac changes over time.

That means there are now two sets of dates for your birth sign. The *tropical dates* are the original Babylonian dates; the *sidereal dates* tell you where the Sun actually appears as it moves along its annual path.

For January 5, the tropical signs is **Capricorn** and the sidereal sign is **Sagittarius**.

Sagittarius

Tropical November 23 to December 21
Sidereal December 16 to January 14

The centaur (half-man, half-horse) Chiron was famous as a healer and as an archer. He tutored Achilles, Jason (of Argonaut fame), and Hercules. Unfortunately for Chiron, Hercules accidentally shot him with an arrow that had been dipped in hydra poison. He was unable to find a cure, so gave up his immortality to free Prometheus, and died. In recognition of his sacrifice, Zeus placed him among the stars.

In astrology, Sagittarians are known for their independence and craving for adventure and excitement. They are encouraging and kind, but sometimes lack commitment. They are supposed to be compatible with Aries, Leo, and Libra, but not with Taurus, Scorpio, or Capricorn.

Capricorn

Tropical December 22 to January 20
Sidereal January 15 to February 14

The origins of the constellation Capricorn date back to Sumeria and Babylonia. Based on Enki, the Sumerian god of wisdom and waters, Capricorn has the head and upper body of a mountain goat and the lower body and tail of a fish. The mountain goat represents ambition and intelligence, the fish represents passion and spirituality.

An earth sign, Capricorn is ruled by the planet Saturn. They are often thought to be responsible, patient, ambitious and loyal, but can sometimes be seen as conceited, distrusting, and unimaginative. Capricornians are supposed to be compatible with Taurus, Pisces, and Virgo, but not with Aries, Sagittarius, or Leo.

Illustration by Edward Penfield

What Day of the Week is January 5?

On what day of the week does January 5 fall?

Surprisingly, this isn't an easy question. Because the calendar year is 365 days long (366 in leap years), it doesn't divide evenly by the seven days of the week.

Also, the Earth goes around the Sun in about 365-1/4 days, so a calendar tends to drift over time. That's why the same date falls on different weekdays in different years.

This is made even more complicated by a change in calendars that took place in 1582. Our modern calendar has its roots in ancient Rome, in a calendar reform conducted by Julius Caesar. Caesar commissioned mathematicians to attack the problem, and they came up with the idea of leap years, and thus standardized the calendar for centuries to come. This was called the Julian calendar.

Over time, however, the small errors in Caesar's calculation compounded. That's why Pope Gregory XIII commissioned the Gregorian calendar, used in most of the world today. Some countries converted in 1582, when the calendar was first developed; some converted later; other still haven't changed.

Gregorian and Julian aren't the only types of calendars. The Hebrew year, the Islamic year, and many other calendars are used in different parts of the world and among different people.

You can convert Gregorian dates to other calendars, including the Hebrew calendar, the Islamic calendar, and even the Mayan calendar by visiting the Fourmilab Calendar Converter at http://www.fourmilab.ch/documents/calendar/.

Chinese calendar systems are quite complex and have changed several times; a full discussion is far beyond the scope of this book. If you're interested, you can find information here: http://www.hermetic.ch/cal_stud/chinese_cal.htm.

On Names and Dates

Historians use "CE" (Common Era) and "BCE" (Before the Common Era) instead of the more common "AD" (Anno Domini, or Year of Our Lord) and "BC" (Before Christ), reflecting the fact that the year-numbering system established by the Gregorian calendar is used throughout the world in many countries not culturally Christian.

The CE/BCE designation dates back to at least 1708, and has been adopted as a standard by the United Nations and the Universal Postal Union. Because this series of books covers events and people of all nations and cultures, we use the CE/BCE terms.

The abbreviation "O.S." ("Old Style") on some dates refers to the fact that the Russian Empire did not switch from the Julian to the Gregorian calendar at the same time as the rest of Europe, and therefore some figures and events have two dates.

Also, in the Julian calendar in England in the 16th century, the year began on March 25 rather than January 1. To avoid confusion with Gregorian dates, dates between January and March were often written using both years.

People and events whose original names are not in the Western alphabet have their native names (where possible) in the appropriate script shown in parenthesis. If you are using an e-reader to access an electronic version of this book, all characters don't always display on all devices.

A 50-year brass perpetual calendar.

Quote of the Day

"Time is an illusion, lunchtime doubly so."

Douglas Adams,
from *The Hitchhiker's Guide to the Galaxy*

Notes
and
Credits

THER
ACI
MAGNA

Timespinner
Press

Cartoon by John T. McCutcheon

Copyright, Credit, and Contact

Follow Us

Our blog "This Day in History" (http://
timespinnerpress.com/this-day-in-history/) features short
articles on events and people associated with each day, and
updates several times each week. Also subscribe to the
"Quote of the Day" at http://timespinnerpress.com/quote-
of-the-day/. You can get daily links by following us on
Facebook at TimespinnerPress, or on Twitter as
@sidewisethinker.

Contact Us

Find an error or a format problem? Want information about
the series, about us, or about when the volume for your
special day might be available? Please email us at
editor@timespinnerpress.com. (We also take requests if your
special day isn't yet complete. Please give us at least six
weeks' notice if possible.)

Sources

We owe a great debt to Wikipedia, which is our first stop for
research. We attempt to make independent confirmation of
all important dates and facts through a variety of other
sources.

Other sources we frequently use include the Library of
Congress; "on this day" listings from *Encyclopedia Britannica*,
the *New York Times*, and the BBC; Omniglot for the names of
months in other languages; *Chase's Calendar of Events;* and, of
course, the always essential Google.

All art and photographs are either in the public domain, used under a Creative Commons license, or with a "fair use" justification, and most frequently come from Wikimedia Commons and the Library of Congress Prints and Photographs Division.

Attribution is provided where possible, or as requested by the copyright owner, or when there is particular historical significance, listed below. For information about any particular illustration or photograph, please contact us.

Credits

- The cover photograph of the Golden Gate Bridge was taken in 2012 by "Francis1203," and is used here under CC BY-SA 3.0.

- The illustration of the month of January used on the back cover is from the French Gothic illuminated manuscript *Les Très Riches Heures du duc de Berry* by the Limbourg Brothers, Jean Colombe, and an intermediate painter whose name is lost to history.

- The box graphic used on the first page is from a 1916 pamphlet entitled "Divorce versus Democracy" authored by G. K. Chesterton, originally published in London by the Society of St. Peter and St. Paul. It is in the public domain in the US because it was published prior to 1923, and is in the public domain in all countries (including the country of origin) in which the copyright time is the author's life plus 70 years or less.

- The graphic design for the section pages in this book is from a design originally created for a pharmacy label. It is from Wellcome Images (ICV No 11073, photo V0010813), and is used here under CC BY-SA 4.0.

- The dry point etching of the Golden Gate Bridge is by Chesley Bonestell, and originally appeared in the August 1933 issue of *The Architect and Engineer*. There are no known copyright restrictions on this image.

- The photograph of the USS *Kearsarge* (CVA-33) passing under the Golden Gate Bridge is in the public domain as an official US Navy photograph.

- The photograph of the Golden Gate Bridge in the interior of this book was taken in 1984 as part of the Historic American Engineering Record, created by the National Park Service and available from the Library of Congress Prints and Photographs Division (digital ID hhh.ca1355). It is in the public domain as a work created by an employee of the US federal government as part of that person's official duties.

- The front page of the 23 December 1894 issue of *Le Petit Journal* is in the public domain because its copyright has expired. The illustration from the court martial of Alfred Dreyfus is by Henri Meyer.

- The photograph of Nellie Tayloe Ross is from the George Grantham Bain Collection at the Library of Congress (ggbain.29524). It is in the public domain because it was first published prior to January 1, 1923.

- The 2011 photograph of an Egg McMuffin breakfast sandwich was taken by Evan-Amos for Vanamo Media, who released the work into the public domain. Egg McMuffin is a trademark of the McDonald's Corporation, and no challenge to that trademark status is intended.

- The 1971 photograph of Zulfikar Ali Bhutto is courtesy of the Dutch National Archives (Bestanddeelnummer 925-2557) and is used here under CC BY-SA 3.0 Netherlands.

- The 1931 photograph of Wiley Post and Harold Gatty is courtesy of the German Federal Archives (Bundesarchiv Bild 102-11928) and is used here under CC BY-SA 3.0. The photograph has been cropped for this use.

- The painting of Stephen Decatur is by John Wesley Jarvis (1780-1840) and is part of the US Naval Academy Museum Collection. It is in the public domain because its copyright has expired.

- The 1955 portrait photograph of Alvin Ailey is by Carl Van Vechten as part of his "Creative Americans" series, and is in the public domain because of the deed of gift to the Library of Congress (digital ID van.5a51612).

- The 2012 photograph of Diane Keaton was made available by Diane Keaton under CC BY-SA 3.0.

- The 1960 publicity photograph from *Captain Kangaroo* and the 1971 photo from *Sonny and Cher* are both in the public domain because they were published in the United States between 1923 and 1977 without a copyright notice. Traditionally, publicity photographs are not copyrighted because of the way in which they are intended to be used.

- The photograph of Agnes von Kurowsky was made available by the Hemingway Foundation under CC BY-SA 2.5. The photograph has been cropped for this use.

- The image of Dorothy Levitt is from the frontispiece to her book *The Woman and the Car,* and is in the public domain because its copyright has expired.

- The photograph of Bob Caruthers is in the public doXXain because it was first published prior to January 1, 1923, and any copyright has expired.

- The 1919 photograph of Calvin Coolidge is in the public domain because it was first published in the United States prior to 1923. It is from the Library of Congress Prints and Photographs Division (cph.3g10777).

- The photograph of Amy Johnson is in the public domain as a work created by an employee of the government of the United Kingdom.

- The 1909 photograph from the Nimrod Expedition to the Antarctic is from the archive of the Alfred Wegener Institute for Polar and Marine Research, and is in the public domain because its copyright has expired.

- The 1910 photograph of Mistinguett and Maurice Chevalier was taken by François Vals. It is in the public domain in its country of origin and in all countries and areas where the copyright term is life plus 70 years or less.

- The photograph of George Washington Carver was taken circa 1910, and can be found in the collection of the Tuskegee University Archives and Museum. It is in the public domain because it was first published in the United States prior to January 1, 1923.

- The 1933 Goudey baseball cards of Rogers Hornsby and Walter "Rabbit" Maranville are in the public domain because it was published in the United States between 1923 and 1963 and although there may or may not have been a copyright notice, the copyright was not renewed.

- The song poster for "The Twelve Days of Christmas" was created in 2012 by Xavier Romero-Frias, and is used here under CC BY-SA 3.0.

- The painting *January* is from the calendar book *Festkalender* by Hans Thoma. It is in the pubic domain because its copyright has expired.

- The 1968 USSR postage stamp "Prospecting Geologist with Found Diamond and Red Crystals-Pyropes (Garnets)" is not an object of copyright according to Part IV of Civil Code No. 230-FZ of the Russian Federation (2006).

- The 1886 painting "Vase with Red and White Carnations on a Yellow Background" by Vincent Van Gogh is in the public domain because its copyright has expired.

- The German New Year's greeting card was made circa 1900. It is in the public domain because its copyright has expired.

- The 2006 photograph of a red plum blossom (*prunus mume*) was taken by Frank Gualtieri, who released the photograph into the public domain.

- The illustration of camellias by Clara Maria Pope is from Samuel Curtis' *Monograph on the Genus Camellia*, published in 1819. It is in the public domain because its copyright has expired.

- The photograph of a person reading a braille book was taken by Antonio X. Alonso in 2009. It is used here under CC BY-SA 2.0.

- The celestial sphere is from *Scenography of the Ptolemaic Cosmography*, by Johannes van Loon, based on Andreas Cellarius's *Harmonia Macrocosmica*, 1660. It is in the public domain because its copyright has expired.

- The 1906 automobile calendar is by Edward Penfield, and is in the collection of the Library of Congress Prints and Photographs Division. It is in the public domain because its copyright has expired.

- The 50-year perpetual calendar photograph is in the public domain.

- The cartoon by John T. McCutcheon is from his 1905 collection *The Mysterious Stranger and Other Cartoons by John T. McCutcheon*. It is in the public domain because its copyright has expired.

Michael Dobson

License Description and Terms

Aside from material purely in the public domain, photographs and other material in this book are used under specific licenses permitting free use, usually with an attribution requirement. For full text and terms of these licenses, click or enter the appropriate links below. If you believe there is an error in the copyright status or attribution of any of these images, please email us.

- Creative Commons Attribution 2.0 Generic (CC-BY 2.0): http://creativecommons.org/licenses/by/2.0/deed.en

- Creative Commons Attribution-Share Alike 3.0 Generic (CC-BY-SA 3.0): http://creativecommons.org/licenses/by-sa/3.0/

- Creative Commons Attribution-Share Alike 2.5 Generic (CC-BY-SA 2.5): http://creativecommons.org/licenses/by-sa/2.5/deed.en

- Creative Commons Attribution-Share Alike 2.0 Generic (CC-BY-SA 2.0): http://creativecommons.org/licenses/by/2.0/deed.en

- Creative Commons Attribution-Share Alike 1.0 Generic (CC-BY-SA 1.0): http://creativecommons.org/licenses/by-sa/1.0/deed.en

- CC0 1.0 Universal (CC0 1.0) Public Domain Dedication (CC0 1.0) http://creativecommons.org/publicdomain/zero/1.0/deed.en

- GNU Free Documentation License (GFDL): http://en.wikipedia.org/wiki/Wikipedia:Text_of_the_GNU_Free_Documentation_License

Timespinner
Press

Other Books from Timespinner Press

The Story of a Special Day
Michael Dobson

A series of (eventually) 366 volumes covering everything that happened on your special day! Events, births, deaths, quotes, holidays, and much more. It's like a birthday card they'll never throw away!

US$7.95 print / US$2.99 ebook.

From Plassey to Pakistan
Humayun Mirza

The history of British Colonial India and the formation of Pakistan from the unique perspective of the son of Pakistan's first president and last of the royal line of Bengal, Bihar, and Orissa! This unique historical document tells the inside story of this distinguished family, including the detailed story of the coup that toppled his father from power!

US$27.95 print

A Whole New Navy: America's War in the Pacific

Miles Durr

The most comprehensive and detailed description of America's naval war in the Pacific ever—every battle, every ship, every task force and every task group from Pearl Harbor through the Japanese surrender! A must-have for the collection of every World War II buff!

US$29.95 print

Improbable History: The Weird, the Obscure, and the Strangely Important

edited by Michael Dobson

From the birth of Western civilization to the rescue of Apollo 13, from the Leaning Tower of Pisa to Florence's Duomo, history has often turned on small, improbable details. Whatever happened to the ancient Samaritan people? Why did a fortuitous rainstorm allow the British to conquer India? How did an air raid in Italy lead to the development of chemotherapy? What happened when Albert Einstein met Adolf Hitler on the streets of Berlin? How did the Japanese manage to attack the US mainland using balloons? A cast of award-winning writers tackle some of the strangest tales in history!

US$19.95 print

www.ingramcontent.com/pod-product-compliance
Lightning Source LLC
Chambersburg PA
CBHW050426290526
45786CB00003B/1416